Fruitcake or Bearing Fruit

Vicky Ash

Copyright © Vicky Ash 2025

All rights reserved

No part of this book may be reproduced, or stored in a retrieval system, or transmitted in any form or by any means, electronic, mechanical, photocopying, recording, or otherwise, without express written permission of the publisher

> **❝** It is an abuser's dream come true to be labeled the good one and to accuse their victims of their own guilt and own crimes—and also to call the healthy person mentally ill.
>
> - Dr. Bandy X. Lee

Trigger Warning
This story may contain descriptions of physical and sexual violence that some survivors may find particularly upsetting. Please consider your triggers and well-being before reading past this point.

Dedication

I dedicate this book to my Heavenly Father,
who has called me by name Vicky - to be Victorious!
To my Lord and Saviour, Jesus Christ,
who died at Calvary to set me free.
To the precious Holy Spirit,
who continues to empower me
to fulfil my destiny in Christ...

To Him be the glory, forever and ever.
Amen

Foreword

Vicky Ash is a committed Christian who is married with three adult children, including a daughter with additional needs. She is a victor of, and campaigns tirelessly for, the exposure of Satanic Ritual Abuse (SRA), which is endemic in our society today. As a qualified beauty therapist and fitness instructor, God has led her to run a Christian ministry which outreaches to the community.

She warns of the hidden dangers of the occult associated with certain treatments and other religious practices infiltrating the business of beauty therapy today.

She is also anointed to run Fit for Life, a weekly prayer meeting and free lunch for anyone who is drawn by God to attend.

In 2009, after 7 years of service, the ministry won a Pride Award. Her first book has been written from the heart and with no apology for the humorous excerpts found in it. She believes that we must laugh in the face of adversity, trusting that the joy of the Lord is our strength (Nehemiah 8:10).

Author's Note

I would have preferred to have written a completely factual book but sadly the law as it stands prevents me from doing that. Instead, I have written this as a novel with my lifetime experiences and research. This novel accurately portrays how Systemic Abuse occurs affecting both individuals and families often with the connivance of the state.

Sadly, many whistleblowers are silenced and serving prison sentences.

In recent years comments have been put on my social media by people who know me well confirming the truth:

"Oh Lord what a dreadful situation. These dreadful acts have taken place for many many years and no mistake still takes place to this day by people one would never expect. Dreadful, dreadful."

The stories in this book reflect the author's recollection of events. Some names, locations, and identifying characteristics have been changed to protect the privacy of those depicted.

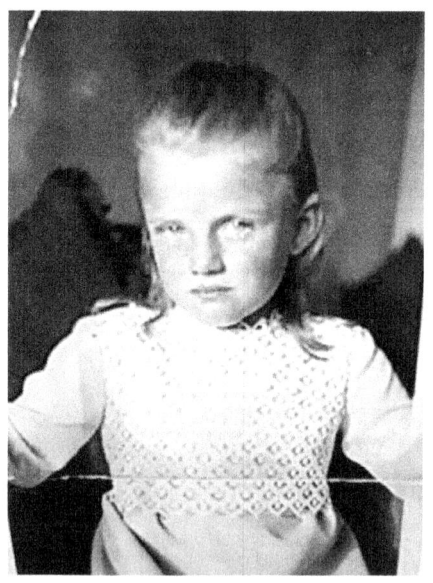

Contents

Introduction God Calls 1

Chapter 1 Frozen Fruit 7

Chapter 2 Confusion and Control 13

Chapter 3 Unfolding Plans with a Tuna Fish Sandwich 19

Chapter 4 Help is at Hand 25

Chapter 5 Blessings and Babies 33

Chapter 6 Mother's Role 39

Chapter 7 More Grace for the Race 47

Chapter 8 God's Timing 53

Chapter 9 Unique 65

Chapter 10 God Promises, God Saves 75

Chapter 11 Ministry Flourishes 81

Chapter 12 Eagles Nest 91

Chapter 13 Uncovered Memories 97

Chapter 14 Letting Go 103

Chapter 15 Hope and Glory 109

Last Word 113

Acknowledgements 115

Introduction
God Calls

Fruitcake or Fruit-bearer?

After reading my story, I hope you'll decide whether my life resembles a *fruitcake* to the world or one that *bears fruit* in the Kingdom of God.

Sarcastically, being a 'fruitcake' in the world's eyes often implies someone is mentally ill. But, in God's Kingdom, 'bearing fruit in Christ' presents the image of Jesus as the Vine and His followers as those who remain in the Vine. Jesus is the Way, the Truth, and the Life. A vine is planted with the sole purpose of producing and bearing fruit. Similarly, I believe we are planted and rooted in God's vineyard to bear fruit.

(John 15:NIV) I pray that as you read my story, you too will come to the Vine to "taste and see that God is good". (Psalm 34:8 NIV)

Life's journey often brings us face-to-face with ourselves, our relationships, and our God. For me, that moment came one day in a Starbucks Coffee Shop. It felt as though I was speaking directly to God about writing this book. There it was, bold as day - the first page of a book, with a commission to begin writing that day, twelve years ago.

So urgent was the mission He would wake me in the early hours.

I love how God does that - breaking into my life with prophetic signs, like those promised in Joel 2:28:

I will pour out my Spirit on all people. Your sons and daughters will prophesy, your old men will dream dreams, your young men will see visions.

God, through His Holy Spirit, surprises me at the most unexpected moments, nudging me gently yet unmistakably in His direction.

"Alright, Lord," I asked then, "how do I begin to share this incredible journey of stepping into my destiny with You?"

Immediately, I heard the words of a Lionel Richie song: "You are my destiny, you are my one and only, you gave that joy to me when my whole life was lonely."

As Christians, we are called to forgive our enemies so that we ourselves might find holistic healing and restoration. But that process begins with the painful step of facing and telling the truth. Ultimately, it is Jesus - the Truth - who sets us free (John 8:32).

I spent much of my early life wrestling with inner demons I couldn't understand. Unbeknownst to me, these dark forces had sinister roots, buried deep in my past. My family knew I had issues. Looking back, I recall a day when my older brother, visited me from abroad. I remember him standing in my kitchen and saying something I never expected: "The only way you'll ever get better, is to go to church."

There was such raw emotion in his voice. His words puzzled me.

"What on earth would I want to go to church for? Where was God when we were children?" I shot back mockingly.

Yet, despite my sarcasm, I couldn't ignore the sincerity in his eyes. The man before me, that had sought psychiatry himself before moving away was so much calmer than I remembered. The change was so positive that it drew me to listen.

"Don't you know that Jesus died on the cross for you?" he asked.

Tears filled his eyes. I thought he had gone mad, but I couldn't deny the point he made. I had tried everything else - counselling, spiritual healing - yet nothing worked long term. What did I have to lose? I decided I would go to church the following Sunday to see if this God could do anything for me.

That Sunday, I walked into church. From that moment, every visit overwhelmed me with an indescribable presence that always reduced me to tears. On the outside, I appeared composed, rather like a swan gliding serenely across a lake, but underneath, my legs were paddling frantically against a tide that wanted to pull me under. The battle for my soul had begun, and only God knew The Way to freedom.

I sat at the back of the congregation, one eye open and one shut, wondering why everyone else was there and what some of them 'were on'. I could see a light in some people, a connection to something greater that I didn't have. Without words, their joy and peace shone. I longed for it.

Yet, suspicion would always creep back in. "Ahaa here comes the collection bag," I thought. "That's what they want - my money. How much does it cost to know this God? Oh, no! Now they're hugging each other, saying 'Peace.' Please don't hug me; surely, that costs something too?"

The word 'love' triggered a flood of painful memories: my father leaving me at the age of 10 at boarding school, speeding away, I remember at this point running after his car, banging on his boot and he jumped out and checked that I hadn't damaged his car. He then dragged me back into the boarding house and said, "Pull yourself together, stop snivelling. Seven years I did in the army." Such hardness of heart. My mother, always preoccupied with golf, even during my school holidays; and my husband, perpetually working away, never fully present.

Then God would break through the walls of my heart again. One particular day, Lionel Richie's song, "Hello," spoke to me: "Hello. Is it ME you're looking for?"

I knew it was God. He was the only One who could fill that void, that gaping hole in my soul aching for unconditional love and acceptance, a place where rejection and abandonment don't exist.

Chapter 1

Frozen Fruit

I had become familiar with that awful loneliness and isolation; that inner voice that was always screaming out "Help!" that drove me into a spiral of alcohol abuse, eating disorders, and exercise addiction. I was in self-destruct mode and hated myself. Always feeling dirty and unclean. I had to stay in control of my environment, so I cleaned the house obsessively. What was wrong with me?

All I knew was that I had very few memories before the age of 14. As I started to uncover them, they emerged slowly, like frozen fruit thawing one by one, each memory slipping free from the frost of years of suppression. As a result, I had to tentatively cope with the truth of my experiences.

Right through my childhood and into my late 20s, I had a recurring dream that I would childishly describe as "a squishy big sausage" coming at me. I would wake up crying and in a hot sweat. Although I regret it, I would often say to my husband that I liked him from the waist up but couldn't bear to look at his anatomy below. I struggled greatly with intimacy and would climb into bed, pulling my nightdress up between my legs to protect myself from "the weapon".

The flashbacks drove me to seek answers, turning to God in desperation. Memories from my childhood started to resurface - disjointed but insistent, like puzzle pieces long buried. The first came from when I was three: my mother meeting someone else and the separation from my father.

She took my brother Nick and I to her parents' home to live. It was a large, beautiful house but I never liked the fact that it backed onto a graveyard. We would spend Sundays with our father, stay overnight and he would take us to school the following morning. I dreaded those occasions when he put me to bed in the room next to my brother. I knew that I couldn't settle and go to sleep because he would come and get me up later. The mattress was hard and cold. I always climbed into bed with my nightie pulled up between my legs trying to protect myself before he came. Insistently he would put his hands under my bedcovers and start tickling me and pull my nightie down. He would carry me to his big 'sweaty' bed. These instances became the foundation of the nightmares I would regularly have of the squishy sausage my childish mind had concocted to make sense of all that he did to me. I had to be very careful not to hurt him and catch it with my teeth!

The next morning, he would kneel before me and fasten my school tie too loosely, saying that I was his "special girl" and that I mustn't tell anyone or I would be in trouble with the police.

I often wonder if my teachers suspected something was wrong. But if they did, no one ever said anything. As a child, I learned that adults either couldn't - or wouldn't - help me, and I carried that belief well into adulthood.

These episodes were interspersed with crueller activities.

One night, he used a poker in front of the fireplace to hurt me in ways that left me unable to sit down in class the next day.

I was taken to the Headteacher of the primary school I attended, who then saw the wounds on my bottom and called my guardians in.

I vividly remember my mother laying me across the bed at my grandmother's house where we lived. She made me count to 10 and on the count of 10 she ripped the plasters off one by one and then replaced them with clean dressings.

In hindsight, it seems astonishing that this could continue to go on as though it was normal.

As a result of the physical internal sexual abuse, my health was seriously affected. I was always constipated, as it was so painful to go to the toilet, I would cross my legs for days in fear of the pain of having to open my bowels. I would regularly be playing out with my friends doing this, as I desperately needed the toilet. My mother and grandmother would see me, and call me inside to assist with bathroom visits to soften my faeces as I screamed in pain.

I remember struggling with constipation at my father's house too and running down the corridor screaming in pain. He came to ask me what was wrong and I remember saying, "It's your fault I can't go to the toilet!"

Bed-wetting followed me into my teenage years, the rubber mat beneath my sheets a source of constant shame. My mother's frustration only deepened my guilt: "It stinks like a farmyard in here!" she'd snap.

Later, this sexual abuse would contribute to urinary tract infections, ovarian cysts, and further gynaecological problems as an adult.

My gag reflex became compromised, an issue which my doctor described as "a nervous cough". But for many years I could never swallow liquid without hesitation or keep my mouth open for too long at the dentist.

How did no one notice and protect me?

Aside from occasional bed-wetting (which was a result of bullying at school), none of my own children displayed any of these symptoms growing up. It became apparent that I had not had a normal childhood.

Chapter 2

Confusion and Control

I adored my father. That might sound strange, given what he did to me, but as his daughter, he held this inexplicable power over me. I desperately wanted to please him, even though I detested the 'games' he regularly forced me to play.

My feelings were tangled and confusing. His attentions made me feel dirty, yet there were moments when my body betrayed me, reacting to the sensations in ways I couldn't understand. It left me questioning myself. Was I to blame? Was I complicit? I pushed those thoughts away, burying the shame deep inside and convincing myself that being his "special girl" made everything acceptable. The anguish of that inner conflict tormented me. How could a child make sense of their body's responses while their mind screamed in protest? That confusion was part of his grooming, a deliberate manipulation that made disclosure terrifying.

I remember behaving inappropriately for my age, often without realising it. I was terrified of my father, especially after he hurt me, but his anger twisted reality. He would blame me, accusing me of causing his actions. "Why do you make me do this?" he'd demand. His words left me bewildered and guilt-ridden, even though I didn't understand what I'd supposedly done wrong.

He was controlling in other ways too. When I was a child, he took me to the barbers who cut all my curls off. I remember being teased relentlessly at Primary School as my friends referred to me as 'the new boy'. Had my father purposely done this to make me look like a boy I wondered?

As I grew older, he'd warn me to "keep my hand on my ha'penny," a crude way of trying to control my relationships with boys. I tried so hard to be "good", but I was seething with anger inside. At boarding school, I began to rebel.

I hated my life.

Despite the rebellion, I wasn't promiscuous. I clung to his warnings, keeping my "hand on my ha'penny, "but I sought attention in other ways. In my late teens I wore flirtatious clothes - anything backless, leather, or above the knee made me feel visible. Yet when boys showed interest, I'd retreat, shy and frigid. I was completely lost in my own identity.

Who was I? My mother called me a tart, and I knew I was hard work for her, but didn't she know why? She wasn't protecting me.

My mind was a battlefield. Conflicting thoughts and emotions overwhelmed me as I constantly tried to make sense of everything.

Due to my extreme weight loss in my teens, I had Amenorrhea which is the absence of menstruation often defined as missing periods. In my early twenties I also developed an ovarian cyst the size of a grapefruit which had to be surgically removed.

Flashbacks were part of my mental landscape but became more frequent when I was pregnant with my first son, Jamie. During therapy I was told that our minds are like a well. We have a subconscious mind and a conscious mind, negative things that happen to us are pushed down into our subconscious mind. When that well becomes full, it starts spilling out into our consciousness which as a result can cause a nervous breakdown.

The memories came unbidden, haunting me. It is documented that with childhood trauma memories are suppressed. I remember my father's twisted pride when Jamie was born. He loved to tell people that Jamie had been "made in Spain" when my husband

and I stayed at his villa. That wickedness only deepened with other crude remarks from his relative saying, "Now we know you do it!"

They took every opportunity to undermine my relationship with my husband. Their mockery and lewd jokes never ceased, and I was branded a prude for refusing to laugh along. Even then, something inside me recognised it was wrong, and I stood my ground.

When Jamie was due to be born, my father conveniently chose to leave the country. Everyone around me seemed anxious, warning me that I might lose the baby. At the time, I couldn't understand their unease, but in hindsight, it made sense given the abuse my body had endured. Fortunately, my labour was relatively short - five hours - and Jamie was placed in my arms, perfect and precious. But instead of joy, I felt immense panic. How could I raise this child when I still felt like a child myself?

I was reminded of the film *The Hand That Rocks the Cradle*. My father had already acquired a cot and a highchair for his house, as though he were preparing to take ownership of Jamie. It felt like my baby had been born for him.

At that time, I was running my first beauty clinic, named after my husband and me. The clinic was located above a shop my father owned, and he expected me to drop Jamie off at his house on

FRUIT CAKE OR BEARING FRUIT

Saturdays before starting my first client at 9am. On the face of it this may have seemed a great help to me, but his motives were clearly not in mine or my baby's best interests.

I was riddled with anxiety and often experienced nausea and the runs, unable to shake the unease about leaving Jamie with him. Yet my memories of the abuse were still locked away, buried so deeply that I couldn't consciously connect them to my dread. My father's control over me remained absolute. His comments, like, "You are nothing without me," and "My sperm made you," continued to dominate my life, eroding any sense of self-worth I tried to build. He even violated boundaries by asking invasive questions about my intimacy with my husband which I felt compelled to tell him.

I had become a beauty therapist in an attempt to make my father proud, but unbeknownst to me, change was on the horizon. One day, I drove past a launderette that was up for sale in the local village. It truly lit up like a beacon - a sense of peace washed over me as though God were guiding me to it. I seized the opportunity to become independent, both personally and professionally. Incredibly, within a week, we sold our home for the asking price, allowing us to make an offer on the launderette, which was promptly accepted.

It was the first step toward breaking free from my father's oppressive control. Little did I know that another Father - one far greater - was about to take charge of my life.

Chapter 3
Unfolding Plans with a Tuna Fish Sandwich

Moving to the launderette felt like a positive shift - a chance to combine my career with being a hands-on mother. Living above the business seemed ideal, especially since my husband often worked away. However, I hadn't anticipated the backlash from the community. Closing the launderette left some neighbours disgruntled, and I could feel their disappointment like a heavy weight. Guilt gnawed at me, and I began questioning my decision, even considering whether I should offer to do their washing to make amends. I overheard that many people doubted that my beauty clinic would last more than six months, but God had other plans.

While life at home and work evolved, my spiritual journey was also progressing. I had made a commitment to my faith and became 'Born Again' by repenting of my sin and asking the Holy Spirit to come into my life. It wasn't easy, and often it didn't make much sense, but I clung to the hope of recovery and restoration. I would join in saying the 'Lord's Prayer' but when it came to the area of forgiveness, I could only be honest as I said, "forgive me my trespasses as I ...try ... to forgive those who have trespassed against me." This was a very painful area that I was going to have to walk through.

One of the deacons at the church I attended prophesied that our future ministry would be a beacon of light for the Lord and indeed it had 'lit' up when I first drove past it. Those words gave me strength to persevere, though I frequently struggled within the church environment. I didn't realise it at the time, but the Holy Spirit was at work, exposing the darkness that had taken root in my life.

The word "sin" became a trigger. I'd find myself scurrying to hide under the church pews, and whenever I approached the altar for Communion, my body would tremble violently. I knew I needed God, but I also had a paralysing fear of His punishment. I couldn't contain the pain inside me any longer and often found myself crying uncontrollably in church.

FRUIT CAKE OR BEARING FRUIT

Some members of the congregation viewed my behaviour as attention-seeking or overly dramatic, but for me, it was raw and real. If I couldn't be honest with God, who knew the whole truth about my life, where else could I go?

I was desperate to live, not just exist, and I was determined to break free from the nightmare that had trapped me for so long.

On one occasion I went to an informal service in the evening at our local Church. After the singing the vicar asked if anyone had a word or picture for us. The worship leader had a picture of a large shield and was describing its appearance. I looked around at everyone, angrily mocking to see if anyone reacted to it but there was no response.

I thought 'Hoorah Henry, he's seen a shield, now what do we all do?

We continued in the service and then the vicar said, "Now bring your prayers individually to God."

I bowed my head with my elbows on my knees and prayed, "If You're there, God, just answer me one question, why does evil seemingly have so much power in the world?"

Immediately I felt a sensation like pins and needles shoot up both my arms and heard an audible voice that said, "Not if you wear your shield!"

I burst into tears as it was such an overwhelming encounter reminding me of the scripture in Ephesians 6:16-17.

In addition to all this, take up the shield of faith, with which you can extinguish all the flaming arrows of the evil one.

The worship leader confirmed to me that he felt that the picture God had given, was indeed for me.

The time came when I knew I needed to confront my father. The memories were surfacing faster now, and the weight of what I'd endured became impossible to ignore, especially with my responsibility to protect Jamie. I decided to invite my father over for lunch.

I know it might sound strange, but I carefully prepared a tuna fish sandwich - his favourite. In my mind, everything had to be just right. Even then, I was still trying to please him.

When he arrived, I was struck by how pale he looked. I was certain he suspected this moment was coming. He knew that I had been struggling and seeking help. I began hesitantly, explaining that I was unwell and needed to get better. Then, with trembling words, I told him that during therapy I remembered what he had done to me as a child.

FRUIT CAKE OR BEARING FRUIT

His reaction was immediate - aggressive and defensive. He dragged my stepmother, Gwen, into the conversation, spitting out bitter accusations: "Who are you going to believe after all I've done for you? Gwen says you've always been jealous of her."

I was in shock, watching him pace the kitchen as his guilt and anger consumed him. I hadn't invited him there to get him into trouble. All I wanted was for him to say he was sorry so I could begin to heal. But he couldn't. He kept rubbing his hands together, turning towards me as if to help, then retreating in frustration. It was as though he was at war with himself.

Finally, I broke. I slid to the floor, leaning against the kitchen wall, tears streaming down my face. "Please leave this house," I sobbed. "You'll never see me or my child again."

He left, and needless to say that the tuna fish sandwich remained untouched.

The following day, Gwen called me. Her words were chilling: "It's not your father who's the problem. It's your brother. We've got dates, times, and places."

I was floored. What had my brother got to do with anything? A calendar? Were they keeping a record of these horrific events? My mind reeled at the thought.

Chapter 4
Help is at Hand

Jamie was attending a local nursery school run by a wonderful woman named Vera Lomas. I remember on our first meeting of accepting a place at the nursery saying that if she did her job and looked after my child, I would do mine and look after her.

Vera wasn't just the proprietor; she was also a regular client of mine, coming in for beauty treatments. Over time, she became much more than a client - she became a treasured, lifelong friend.

At a time when I was still learning the ropes of motherhood, Vera was a Godsend. She taught me so much about raising children, with her approach rooted in unconditional love and patience. She never judged where I was in my journey; instead, she met me where I was and encouraged me to grow. I began applying the same principles to my parenting that Vera used at her nursery, and it made such a difference in my life. I remember her beautiful words, "Take it where your child is at not where you are at." That was always the ethos of life at her nursery school and it was a privilege to witness the children there truly thrive.

Vera had an uncanny ability to sense my distress. She noticed how I'd become overwhelmed if I heard a child crying at the nursery. She reassured me that I didn't need to stress about forcing my child at tea-time because he had adequate meals earlier. She even showed up at my house during my panic attacks, helping me cope when I felt I couldn't manage. Vera's nursery provided the stability my child needed while I faced the turmoil in my own life.

Thursday evenings became a highlight for me, as Vera came in for her weekly beauty treatment. It was during these appointments that she witnessed my odd behaviour. I'd ride my exercise bike religiously, even sometimes during her treatments and she'd see me pop across the road to the off-licence for a litre of wine before she left. Vera never criticised or judged; she simply listened as I poured out the trauma I was living through. Week after week, she offered her unwavering support.

Some friends only walk with you for a season, but Vera was a friend for life. God gave her the grace to stand by me every second of every day, no matter how challenging things became. I saw through her what the

FRUIT CAKE OR BEARING FRUIT

Bible calls *"a very present help in time of trouble"* (Psalm 46:1). She was never too tired or distracted to be there for me. Through her, I witnessed the true nature of God's love, and I often wondered how I could ever repay her for her kindness.

God's love was reflected in Vera's actions. Her consistent presence in my life led me to ask deeper questions about God and Jesus. I'd heard about the crucifixion, but I didn't fully understand why Jesus had died for me or what it had achieved. As always, God had a way of answering my questions in the most unexpected ways.

It was Easter when I came across a television documentary about a man who needed stem cell replacement therapy to survive. His sister turned out to be a perfect match and underwent surgery to donate her stem cells. When asked about the pain she endured for her brother, she said, "I would die for my brother."

Her brother, in turn, said, "How can I ever repay her for giving me life?"

As I watched, I heard the Lord speak to me. He said, "I didn't have an anaesthetic, and I didn't just give my stem cells - I gave my whole body on the cross as your perfect donor. I am not a way, a truth, or a life; I am THE WAY, THE TRUTH, and THE LIFE."

This revelation was life changing. Just as there are physical laws for donor matching, there are spiritual laws for salvation, and Jesus is the perfect match for all of us. He is the only way to eternal life.

As my relationship with God deepened, I became more aware of my shortcomings. I read 1 John 5:3, which says, *"In fact, this is love for God: to keep His commands. And His commands are not burdensome."* My immediate reaction was to protest: "They feel very burdensome because I can't obey them!" But God had an answer for me: "That's because you don't know Me. When you know Me, you will love Me."

The chorus of a song began to echo in my mind:

Getting to know you,
Getting to know all about you,
Getting to like you,
Getting to hope you like me.

How incredible it was to realise that the song was from *The King and I*, and Scripture tells us that Jesus is the King.

Despite this growing understanding, I continued to struggle. I knew it was wrong to get drunk, but I couldn't seem to stop. I attended AA meetings regularly and followed the 12-step programme, which emphasises spiritual help. I remember one night crying out to God: "If You want me to stop drinking, please

FRUIT CAKE OR BEARING FRUIT

tell me." I heard the words "Ephesians 5" and looked it up in my Bible. It read, *"Do not get drunk with wine, which will ruin you; instead, be filled with the Spirit"*(Ephesians 5:18).

I remember thinking "Can I have a brandy, then?"

I also grumbled about how unfair it was to try to give up drinking while living opposite a liquor store. God had a reply for that too: "If you can't get over this hurdle, you won't get over what's ahead."

I eventually managed to stop drinking during the week, which was a significant improvement and I encountered the peace and freedom this brought. However, on Saturday nights, I still 'treated' myself to a drink, reasoning that wine was made from grapes, and fruit was good for me. I was living in self-deception.

Sundays were always a battle. I'd wake up with suicidal thoughts feeling separated from God and wrestled with them on the way to church. I desperately wanted to draw closer to God, but I didn't know how.

Then, out of the blue, I was invited to my neighbour's baptism at the local Methodist church. The sermon was about the Holy Spirit burning like a flame inside us when we are born again. The minister warned not to do anything to extinguish that flame. I instantly pictured myself getting drunk and the flame within me going out. I felt the Lord say, "Now choose."

I then had the revelation that this issue was separating me from Him.

I pleaded with Him, "I can't give it up on my own. Please help me." From that moment, I began seeing signs on the liquor store's windows: "Spirits… distilled in hell". "Cellar" I imagined falling into a pit every time I drank, and understood the term "demon drink" in a new light.

The turning point came when I sought help from a Christian organisation for those battling addiction. I attended a weekly evening meeting for fellowship and prayer ministry. I will never forget walking into the leader's house and seeing a huge hole in the wall between the kitchen and lounge to allow more people to get in. This is faith in action, like the story in the Bible of the lame man brought to Jesus for healing on a stretcher. His friends made a hole in the roof to get him in because they were so determined to help him.

I would regularly say, "Don't talk to me about Jesus; show Him to me!" This act of faith certainly did.

I've come to realise that all addictions are, at their core, a disorder of worship. If God isn't at the centre of your life, you end up filling your empty heart by running to the wrong things to alleviate the pain.

At one meeting, I asked for prayer about whether I should report my father to the police. The group advised against it, prioritising my safety and that of my family. However, I couldn't find peace with that decision and asked God for clarity. That night, I heard the words "James 2." Thinking it might concern my son Jamie, I rushed upstairs to check on him, only to find him perfectly fine. Then I realised it was the Bible passage I needed. I opened to James 2:17: *"Faith by itself, if it is not accompanied by action, is dead."* I knew what I had to do.

I believed that that was the confirmation of Gods answer to me, and I decided to go to the police. Soon after that, I met with my local Member of Parliament (MP). This led to a connection with the founder of Childwatch an organisation which helped sexually abused children. She instructed me to contact the CID (Criminal Investigation Department) and also put me in touch with two of her counsellors to support me.

Chapter 5

Blessings and Babies

My husband and I had been trying for a second child for some time, when I began having a recurring dream about getting married in a church. We had married in a register office as we had lived together. Even before I came to faith, I had always felt that it would be hypocritical to wear white in a church wedding. My father had discouraged the idea of a church ceremony as well, even to the extent of making his opinion known several times publicly. However, the church dream was persistent, and it stirred something in me.

I spoke to my vicar about it, and he said that God often speaks to us through dreams. He advised us to have our marriage blessed in church. It was the right thing to do, so my husband and I arranged a blessing ceremony for 21 October.

We invited my remaining family to attend and I was confused and hurt by their lack of enthusiasm.

They declined to come and didn't send any acknowledgement of our celebration. However, some of our friends showed up to support us. Nine months later, on 21st July, our second son, Brandon, was born.

Brandon's birth was a traumatic experience. I was induced and in labour for thirteen hours. At the height of it, I had flashbacks that overwhelmed me with a sense of the baby being a forced delivery. I was hysterical, shouting things like, "Kill me and the baby!" and "I'm having an alien!"

Looking back, I feel deeply for Brandon, entering the world amid such chaos and curses. I've since explained to him that those words weren't spoken from my heart but from a place of sheer panic and trauma. Yet at the time, it felt like I was experiencing something unnatural, as though my body were rebelling against me. This triggered the trauma of my previous abortion which I was yet to deal with - a memory I couldn't quite grasp but that haunted me in the shadows.

After Brandon was born, my mother sat at the end of my hospital bed and said something very controlling: "This baby is going to change your life. Forget the past and concentrate on Brandon." Her words felt more like an order than encouragement.

FRUIT CAKE OR BEARING FRUIT

How could I possibly forget the past? She knew the journey to reveal the truth that I was on, which was obviously very threatening for her. My life felt like an open wound, festering and unhealed. How could I give Brandon the love he deserved when I was still battling my own demons? This too reminded me of Isaiah 1 vs 5-6:

> *"Why should you be beaten anymore? Why do you persist in rebellion? Your whole head is injured, your whole heart afflicted. From the sole of your foot from the top of your head there is no soundness – only wounds and welts and open sores, not cleansed or bandaged or soothed with olive oil."*

I wanted to breastfeed him, just as I had done with Jamie, but my struggles with an eating disorder and alcohol made it a constant battle. I was trapped in the torment of trying to be a good mother while feeling like a broken child myself. Guilt and condemnation tightened their grip on me with every failure.

As I fought for my own freedom, I couldn't ignore the fact that I remembered my father battling his own demons. Denial seemed to be his shield. I witnessed his violent and aggressive behaviour continue unchecked. On one occasion, I saw him beating his dog with a lead. Months later, he criticised me for shouting at my dog, to which I retorted, "At least I don't beat her with a lead!"

He looked me in the eye and said, "What are you talking about? I've never hit my dog in my life." His denial was astonishing.

I thought back to the time he shot at his neighbour's dog because it had wandered onto his land. He showed no remorse, just as he had none for the countless other acts of cruelty I'd seen.

My brother bore the brunt of our father's rage too. Once, when we were on holiday in a hotel lift, we saw a famous actress and my brother began shouting excitedly about her.

Our father suddenly stopped the lift between floors and proceeded to punch him relentlessly. He beat Nick right there in the confined space, leaving us both terrified. At another time Nick and I had gone away on holiday with our swimming teacher. An incident took place where we ran away and consequently our father was called to come and get us. Nick was beaten once again! We'd learned to fear not just him but also his relatives, who were loud, argumentative men. Their frequent shouting matches in the family business were embarrassing for everyone around them. I remembered the Calendars of topless women they hung in their offices which I found very uncomfortable. I once rang one of them to ask if he could describe my father's first house since separating from my mother. I needed confirmation of the flashbacks I was having.

His response was, "stop delving into the past as it will only cause you more pain".

As I reflected on these moments, I couldn't help but think about the anger that was simmering within me. It wasn't surprising, really. The Bible talks about the sins of the fathers carrying on to the third and fourth generation, and I was living proof of that generational curse. This became even more apparent when Brandon, who was being bullied at school, went through a phase of wetting the bed. One day, I stormed into his room, yelling the very words my mother had shouted at me: "It stinks like a farmyard in here!"

The moment the words left my mouth, I clasped my hands over it in shock. I couldn't believe I had repeated her cruelty. It was then that I realised I had to break this cycle of sin. I had to be the one to stop it.

Chapter 6
Mother's Role

My mother has always denied knowing anything about the abuse I suffered as a child, let alone having any involvement in it. Yet, things simply 'don't add up. She would dismiss my concrete memories and attempt to rewrite my personal history.

My stepfather confided in me that he didn't think my mother was telling the truth. He said she had once told him that my father had done bad things to her too when they were married.

Despite this, she became increasingly nervous and controlling, wanting to know my every move. She began rationalising her actions and undermining my attempts to share the truth. "You had such a vivid imagination as a child," she'd say.

One example that stands out is her insistence that the burns I clearly remembered on my bottom were actually a bout of ringworm I'd supposedly caught from the toilet seats at school. I knew that wasn't true as at exactly that time Jamie had ringworm, and his case was completely different. His lesions were very few, painless red circles with pale centres, and they weren't confined to just one area. A topical cream from the family doctor had cleared them up quickly. My wounds, on the other hand, were painful, located only on my bottom, and required scabs to be dressed repeatedly. I knew the difference. My mother also said that I would have scars if this incident had taken place. However, that isn't true. A surface burn can heal completely.

It appeared to me that there was a total lack of appropriate boundaries in our relationship which should have provided me with a sense of security and respect for all parties. Certain topics of conversation around myself felt uncomfortable and invaded my privacy. I have truly struggled all my life in this area. Where were the boundaries in our childhood?

Her behaviour manifested in other, more insidious ways. She often brought in so-called "experts" to intimidate me or refute my claims. At one point, she invited a friend of hers who was a solicitor to our house. That was the first time that I disclosed to her about my father abusing me and she immediately responded with, "Thank God, I thought it was your brother!"

FRUIT CAKE OR BEARING FRUIT

What a statement? My husband was present at the time. The solicitor looked me in the eye and said that if I ever tried to take my father to court, I'd end up in a mental home. Was that threat an attempt to pervert the course of justice?

On another occasion, my mother took me to see a family doctor who was later struck off the medical register. He would sit there smoking during our sessions. At one appointment, he told me that what I was disclosing was "just the tip of the iceberg." Then he added, chillingly, "You'll be asking me next if it's all right to be doing perverted behaviour in your own sex life." Was this truly a professional counselling session? Absolutely not!

At the time, my mother worked as a ward clerk for a gynaecologist, whose children I babysat while he and his wife went out. Oddly, he too was later struck off the medical register. He treated me for yet another ovarian cyst, which required draining.

Before the operation, he examined me at the local hospital. A male trainee and a female nurse were present. He asked me to remove all my clothing and get on the bed. Then, as if it were a normal part of the examination, he asked if my body tan went "all over" and if I would check my own breasts. He opened my legs, turned to the trainee and said, "This is the clitoris, and you don't touch that, or else you'll go to prison." I still remember the alarmed look on the female nurse's face.

I should have reported him to the police straight away. I wonder why he was later struck off the register. That thought haunted me in later years.

After the operation, as the anaesthetic wore off and I was still under its influence, I began shouting in the hospital ward about the abuse I'd endured as a child. The gynaecologist stormed into the ward, pulled the curtains around my bed, and barked at me, "We all know what's happened to you. Stop feeling sorry for yourself!"

His outburst shocked the ward staff, as well as a neighbour who was in another bed nearby. Later, the sister in charge came over to apologise for his behaviour and to check if I was all right. Her kindness helped, but the damage was already done.

Even after the operation, he sent for me to visit his private practice, despite the fact that I was an NHS patient. During the appointment, he urgently advised me to forget the past and get on with living my life. He sat there chain-smoking, pointing to his cigarette as if to justify himself: "Look at me - that's why I smoke."

I couldn't shake the question of why was he so fearfully concerned to silence me?

FRUIT CAKE OR BEARING FRUIT

When I later mentioned to my mother about this incident of his behaviour, she dismissed it saying that he hadn't been threatening at all. How did she know?

My GP once referred me to a psychiatrist for counselling. He administered what he called "The Truth Drug" as part of my treatment. This involved giving me an injection to help me relax and talk about the past. When I later told the police about it, they said they'd never heard of such a thing. I recall that one of my father's neighbours used to drive me to the hospital for these sessions because I was too sedated to drive myself home afterwards.

My vicar was concerned about this treatment and warned me not to continue. He asked me, "When are you going to trust God?" His words made me think deeply, and I prayed for clarity. During my last visit to see the psychiatrist, he recommended that I speak to a reputable solicitor. This solicitor had been instrumental in helping to free a man who had been wrongly convicted and imprisoned for many years for the sexual abuse and ritual murder of a young girl.

When I met with the solicitor, one of the first things he asked me was whether I thought my father might have been involved in snuff films. He explained that a snuff film is a type of video that supposedly shows scenes of real homicide, often luring victims under false pretences to be filmed during their murder. The idea horrified me. He also mentioned knowing a corrupt solicitor who I realised was the one that had previously come to my 'house. Then he said something that stuck with me: "Your story is like *The Stepford Wives* - everyone is involved. One day, this egg is going to break, and you will be called in to give us the goods!" I couldn't help but wonder if that day might come at Easter.

My mother's final attempt to, "sort me out," as she put it, involved taking me to see another local psychiatrist, again in his private, home-based practice, rather than through the NHS. He had also treated a relative of mine who has now tragically passed away. During the session, his anger was palpable. He threatened both of us, warning my mother that he would section me if I didn't stop talking about the abuse I'd suffered. At one point, I found myself crawling around his lounge on my hands and knees, screaming, "I am telling the truth!"

He sent me out of the room to speak privately with my mother. I overheard her pleading with him, "Please don't hurt her - I will deal with her." Why on earth was she so frightened?

Not long after, my mother arranged for me to return for a second appointment with him. This time, he had me lie down on a chaise longue, attempting to hypnotise me. His suggestion was that I imagine all my memories packed into a suitcase and then throw it over a cliff. By God's protection, his attempt at hypnosis failed. I found the whole approach bizarre - wasn't hypnosis supposed to uncover things, not suppress them? The contradiction wasn't lost on me. My mother constantly referred to me as having 'False Memory Syndrome' yet she was the one arranging therapy sessions that she supposedly disagreed with. It was baffling.

Over the years, my mother and stepfather made several visits to pastors who were supporting me. One visit stands out in my memory. My stepfather claimed at that time I was telling people my mother was a witch, even though I had never disclosed such things. It was now becoming obvious they were pre-empting disclosures before they happened, trying to discredit me in advance.

This reminded me too of the constant battle my grandmother had with her mental health. I loved her dearly and would often support her during my school holidays. In her desperation she shared intimate details of her life. She confided in me that she had suffered a stillbirth and wasn't allowed to know where her baby was buried. She resorted to having electric shock treatment to try and get better, however later she tragically took her own life.

The last time I heard from my stepfather was when he reached out, believing my mother was dying. He sent me a text message that read: *Mum in intensive care, v v poorly. Just letting you know, no problem, just another witch gone with a broken heart.*

I responded with this: I am praying that Mum receives Jesus who loves her as I do.

Chapter 7
More Grace for the Race

When Brandon was six, I decided to qualify as a Keep Fit teacher as I spent so much time training. I derived a lot of support from the local community. I held sessions in the local school and band club. The nature of the training also led me to qualify in teaching children, known as a 'Fit Kid' qualification. It was something I enjoyed deeply, and this led me to finding a Keep Fit Studio of my own locally. My husband and I kitted it all out with mirrors on the wall, appropriate flooring and a cafe area. I would run 'Fit Kid' birthday parties; the business was very successful until I started experiencing chronic pain and fatigue.

When on a family holiday in Menorca I ended up bedridden with inflammation all over my face and body. When the doctor came, he said that something more sinister was going on and that he thought I was allergic to sunlight. My husband actually said that I seemed allergic to living! The fight to keep going was relentless.

I also have two other recollections …. once whilst on a skiing holiday with school, being mortified at my face swelling with the wind and secondly being diagnosed with a serious penicillin allergy when I was in my twenties. I was working away at the time and had a very bad reaction turning blue all over. This was so serious that I was told it needed to be written in my medical records so that I was never to be prescribed it again.

I had no resistance against the sunlight or the wind, and my joints swelled and ached terribly because of the exposure. I still wear 'windy glasses' today to prevent my eyes from swelling.

From this time forward, I had frequent visits to my GP who kept insisting that I was just depressed. I knew, though, that it was the relentless pain causing my depression, not the other way around. At the time I was running a successful Beauty Clinic and Keep Fit Studio whilst looking after my children when my husband worked away.

I also had a lot of pain in my jaw which the dentist at the time, said it was my bite. He proceeded to grind some of my teeth down and gave me a bite guard to wear.

FRUIT CAKE OR BEARING FRUIT

I spent a fortune on a chiropractor and finally a physiotherapist who said that I was losing muscle tone even though I exercised frequently which shouldn't be happening.

Out of sheer exhaustion I turned to the Lord again, seeking His guidance on what was wrong. One night, as I watched a television programme called *Ladykillers*, a woman described a condition called Systemic Lupus Erythematosus (SLE). Instantly, I felt a revelation - her symptoms mirrored mine exactly. I wasted no time booking a private appointment with the specialist featured on the programme.

When I arrived at his private surgery, exhaustion weighed so heavily on me that I could scarcely keep my eyes open in the waiting room. During his examination, he remarked that he believed he had identified the problem and proceeded with the necessary blood tests. The results confirmed it: I had SLE. At last, I had a name for what I had been experiencing.

In essence, SLE is a chronic inflammatory condition affecting the joints, including my jaw. It is well-documented in medical literature. Multiple sclerosis is an autoimmune disease that targets the muscles, rheumatoid arthritis affects the bones, and lupus attacks the connective tissue between muscle and bone.

Interestingly, the word *disease originates* from *dis-ease*, a state of imbalance or distress within the body. SLE is often thought to manifest following childhood trauma.

I wasn't imagining things, I wasn't faking it, and I wasn't just seeking attention, as some people had suggested. The immune system should serve to protect whereas mine, in the case of Lupus, was attacking itself. On reflection, it was evident that there was a battle going on in my life between both the physical and spiritual.

I had tried to maintain teaching the Keep Fit - due to being told that there was nothing wrong - by changing the workouts to circuits. That way I didn't have to participate as much, however, it became increasingly unbearable. So, finally I had to stop and close my Keep Fit Studio down, and cancel my Fit Kid sessions. Taking this step was a shattering experience particularly after all the effort and hard work I had put into it.

I was prescribed Methotrexate, given plasma infusions, and other drugs to manage the disease. These treatments provided temporary relief, but nothing more. I remember asking the nurses when I was having plasma infusions to please speed up the drip as I needed to collect my children from school, that's how hectic life was! I knew I needed to press into the Lord for healing and wisdom on how to care for myself. I realised I'd been punishing myself for far too long, neglecting to look after my body the way I should.

I found comfort and conviction in the words from Ephesians:

"After all, no one ever hated their own body, but they feed and care for their body, just as Christ does the church - for we are members of His body" (Ephesians 5:29-31).

Those verses reminded me that I am part of His creation, and I must learn to treat myself with the care and respect that He intends. I would now seek Gods healing.

This hymn inspired me to continue finishing my race:

O Jesus, I have promised
to serve Thee to the end;
be Thou forever near me,
my Master and my Friend;
I shall not fear the battle
if Thou art by my side,
nor wander from the pathway
if Thou wilt be my Guide.
O let me feel Thee near me,
the world is ever near;

VICKY ASH

I see the sights that dazzle,
the tempting sounds I hear;
my foes are ever near me,
around me and within;
but, Jesus, draw Thou nearer,
and shield my soul from sin.
O let me hear Thee speaking
in accents clear and still,
above the storms of passion,
the murmurs of self-will;
O speak to reassure me,
to hasten or control!
O speak, and make me listen,
Thou Guardian of my soul!
O Jesus, Thou hast promised
to all who follow Thee
that where Thou art in glory
there shall Thy servant be;
and, Jesus, I have promised
to serve Thee to the end;
O give me grace to follow,
my Master and my Friend!

Chapter 8
God's Timing

In my impatience with God's healing process, when Brandon was a baby, I attempted to speed things up. I arranged to go to a new age healing retreat to undergo regression therapy. My vicar advised against it, warning me that I could be playing into the Devil's hands. I was livid! How dare he mention the Devil in my house?

Oddly enough, that same week, I received a letter from a Christian healing retreat, offering me a weekend with them. I declined, believing that a fortnight at the original retreat would give me the extended time to deal with so many issues.

How wrong I was.

When my husband, Brandon, and I arrived at the retreat, I felt no peace at all and immediately questioned whether we should even stay. The atmosphere was cold and uninviting, the building was rundown and damp, and I found it bizarre that there were dogs running around with red scarves tied around their necks.

We attended meetings in their so-called *sanctuary*, which was the main spiritual meeting room, and I underwent taped personal therapy sessions in one of their huts, where I recalled my memories. During one session, I spoke about being surrounded by black cloaks and hearing people chanting:

"She has sinned, she has sinned, punish her, punish her, punish her!"

Years later, God showed me a verse of Scripture that put this experience into perspective:

"There is no fear in love. But perfect love drives out fear, because fear has to do with punishment. The one who fears is not made perfect in love." (1 John 4:18)

This verse revealed how the Devil twists even God's Word to groom and enslave people in fear.

During further counselling at the new age retreat, I described a scene with cobbled paving. The counsellors interpreted this as a medieval scene from a past life. I kept insisting it was *me*, with long hair, and I never felt any peace about their conclusions.

Shamefully, I recounted memories of being in mixed saunas with adults, all of us in the nude, watching pornography and playing ' games ' with the adults where I was referred to as being 'The Star of the show'. My father had also taken photographs at these events. A client later informed me that he was known at the golf club to have the largest collection of pornography.

This raw exposure during therapy, without any true healing, felt like it was only making things worse.

My husband stayed for the first week but left after that, and I remained for the second week. One night, during my stay, I don't know how it happened, but I was accidentally locked inside the sanctuary with Brandon overnight. It was a harrowing experience. No one heard me crying and shouting for help. I had to use one of Brandon's nappies as a toilet. The room was so cold that Brandon nearly got pneumonia afterwards. I ended up with one of my dreadful *nervous coughs*.

The entire experience was far from a blessing, and I couldn't stop thinking about my vicar's warning not to attend. He had been right - *Th*is retreat was not run by Christians but by spiritual healers who believed in reincarnation, the concept that the non-physical essence of a living being begins a new lifespan in a different physical form or body after biological death. We are warned in the Bible not to turn to them:

"Do not turn to mediums or seek out spiritists, for you will be defiled by them. I am the Lord your God."(Leviticus 19:31)

Unexpectedly, when I returned home, I heard from the Christian healing ministry again, inviting me for the following weekend. This time, I recognised that God had been intervening all along, trying to help me, but I had free will to choose. The Bible makes this very clear:

"This day I call the heavens and the earth as witnesses against you that I have set before you life and death, blessings and curses. Now choose life, so that you and your children may live and that you may love the Lord your God, listen to his voice, and hold fast to him."(Deuteronomy 30:19-20)

I accepted the second invitation immediately.

I had an appointment scheduled with the police on the Monday after my weekend away, so before I left for the Christian healing ministry on the Friday, I was able to speak to the Founder of Childwatch who had advised me to contact the police.

When I arrived at the Christian healing ministry, the atmosphere was entirely different from my previous retreat experience. It was warm and welcoming - a truly blessed place where God's peace felt tangible. I was assigned two counsellors, one of whom had been a social worker who had come across cases like mine and had experienced being 'silenced' about them. Straight away, they handed me a book titled 'Chasing Satan' describing the author as a brave woman.

I couldn't believe it - was this just a coincidence? I had spoken to same woman that very morning, and they had no way of knowing. I put the book in my suitcase to read later, as I had an intense weekend ahead.

The counselling sessions were gentle, and for the first time, I felt like I wasn't just reliving terrible events but actually beginning to experience the relief that comes with true inner healing. As the Bible says:

"The truth sets us free." (John 8:32)

I was finally on my way to freedom.

In one specific incident, I remember while being abused, that I saw a figure dressed entirely in white standing at the end of the bed.

The figure beckoned to me, saying, *"Come here a minute."*

I felt myself leave my body and looked down at what was happening, completely dissociated from it. Now, I believe that this was Jesus - God's way of protecting me. It reminds me of the Scripture:

"Do not be afraid of those who kill the body but cannot kill the soul. Rather, be afraid of the One who can destroy both soul and body in hell." (Matthew 10:28)

During ministry with the counsellors, I remembered an abusive experience involving my dad, stepmother, and their dachshund. It was a grotesque memory. During their depraved games, they exposed the dog's penis, referring to it as a *"lipstick,"* and held it over my face. They found it amusing to encourage the dog to mount a toy dog, playing this sick game regularly.

As I recounted these perverse bestiality details, the counsellors discerned that what I had been subjected to involved witchcraft.

One of the counsellors said that addressing the spiritual consequences would take time. I felt disappointed when she cautioned, *"You are going to have to walk with the Lord for a long time before you can fully deal with your childhood."* I felt dejected and even angry at the suggestion that I had to serve some sort of apprenticeship with God before He would heal me.

Now, looking back, I understand that God's timing is perfect. At that time, I didn't know Him well enough to trust Him with the revelations that lay ahead.

The counsellors encouraged me with words from Isaiah:

FRUIT CAKE OR BEARING FRUIT

"See, this has touched your lips; your guilt is taken away, and your sin atoned for." Then I heard the voice of the Lord saying, 'Whom shall I send? And who will go for us?'" (Isaiah 6:7-8)

After a long journey through so many forms of treatment, I finally understood that my guilt had been cleansed. I could be that messenger. I said, *"I will go."* The time had come. I was now ready to be interviewed by the CID.

To prepare for the meeting, I decided to go for a walk and prayed that God would help me remember anything relevant to the police enquiry. The officer arrived at 2pm and began asking me lots of questions.

Her attitude was cold, almost accusatory. She asked, "Why has it taken you so long to say anything?"

The interview lasted hours.

At 6pm, I suddenly experienced a vivid flashback right there in front of the officer. I saw the cobblestones and black cloaks that had appeared during the regression therapy, but this time I recognised it all. It was my father's house. The girl in the scene was me as a child, with long hair. My memories weren't fragments of a past life, as had been suggested at the new age place, they were from *this* life. My life. They were my history, my recurring nightmare. I gave these tapes to the police and they were never returned to me.

I remembered how my father, who was never a churchgoer, would attend the church with the farmers at the bottom of his drive for their Harvest Festival. That church was later reported to have been desecrated and used by Satanists in the area. There had been a report about it in the local newspaper.

I felt trapped in a prison of the mind, surrounded by a family that lived in denial, told lies, and falsely accused me. It was torment - enough to drive me to the brink. One day, while walking the dog, I seriously considered taking my own life. I cried out to God in desperation: "How can You look at such evil and injustice and do nothing? If You don't bring corroboration, I can't get through another day of this torment!"

In that moment, I heard the words clearly: "Cook, two, three."

I wondered who might be cooking. As usual, I went to my Bible, searching for answers, and looked through the contents. Sure enough, I found the book of Habakkuk. He was a prophet who had complained about the same thing I was wrestling with why God seemed to delay justice. In chapter 2, verse 3, I read:

FRUIT CAKE OR BEARING FRUIT

Then the Lord replied: "Write down the revelation and make it plain on tablets so that a herald may run with it. For the revelation awaits an appointed time; it speaks of the end and will not prove false. Though it linger, wait for it; it will certainly come and will not delay."
(Habakkuk 2:2-3)

That passage hit me deeply, and I knew God was speaking directly to my situation.

Later that evening, I received a phone call from the counsellors at Childwatch. They had been working with two sisters who described being taken to a house that sounded exactly like my father's. The girls said they were collected in a white Rolls Royce, given orange juice to drink that made them drowsy, and then driven over a cattle grid to a house where they were abused. There is now evidence that drugs are used regularly to groom and abuse.

When I heard this, I felt both horrified and vindicated. I gave Childwatch my wedding album to show the sisters to see if they recognised anyone in the photos. They did. They pointed out my father's relatives. Then they identified my father and said he was the owner of the house.

The police were informed, and they interviewed the sisters separately. Both confirmed their identification of the people and the house, but despite this corroboration, it was classed as contaminated evidence even though I had never met or spoken to them.

I was devastated.

Still, that direct word from Habakkuk was my anchor. It sustained me for the next 20 years and beyond. Whenever I doubted or felt like giving up, I clung to God's promise. I knew justice would come - not out of revenge, because as Scripture says, *"Vengeance is mine," says the Lord* but for the sake of truth. I wanted vindication to set myself and others free.

I was deeply troubled by the impact this had on my children. They were exposed to so much turmoil, often seeing me in distress, and I couldn't shield them from it. They always believed in me, but they were constantly bombarded with letters from their grandparents, who were trying to "groom" them and turn them against me. I had to fight for them, too.

This was never just about me; it was about protecting others. It is often said, "Evil prospers when good men do nothing." In Christian terms, I'd reframe that: "The Devil only prospers when God's people do nothing."

My eldest son, Jamie, once made an observation that still resonates deeply with me. He said my life was like a bike chain and that I had broken the link of abuse for my children. How perceptive he was.

Today, we sing the worship song, *"Break Every Chain,"* and I see how true those words are in my life. I was often told that God had given Jamie the gift of wisdom and that he would be a rock to me. That proved to be so true. As the eldest, Jamie had to grow up too quickly, and I now realise how much of the burden of my journey he carried throughout his childhood especially as his father worked away a lot.

During this turmoil I knew I needed deeper ministry and wasn't free. A lady in Church spoke about a couple who helped people who ministered in the area of deliverance. I decided to contact them. They asked me to send them a picture of myself as they thought that they already knew me. Lo and behold it was the same counsellor that I had seen twelve years previously at the Christian healing ministry who had said *"You are going to have to walk with the Lord for a long time before you can fully deal with your childhood."* Her husband vividly remembered my time there, so much so, that he had been called to continue to keep me in prayer.

Now I was ready to go deeper as this verse reminded me …

Deep calls to deep in the roar of your waterfalls; all your waves and breakers have swept over me (Psalms 42:7-8)

Mr and Mrs White faithfully travelled to minister to me on a regular basis and were instrumental in my healing to freedom in Christ. They also interceded for my husband and children too.

Chapter 9
Unique

I was told that, with my diagnosis of SLE, I probably couldn't have any more children. I didn't fully process this information at the time, as I was simply relieved to finally have an answer to what was wrong with me. So, when Brandon was eight years old, I was completely surprised - and thrilled - to discover I was pregnant again.

At around three months pregnant, I began experiencing vision problems that felt similar to a migraine. After seeing my GP, he sent me urgently to see my SLE specialist, I was diagnosed with a retinal occlusion - a blood clot - in my right eye.

In my research since, I came across information that had never been mentioned to me at the time.

Around one-third of women with lupus have antibodies that may cause blood clots and interfere with the proper functioning of the placenta. This is most likely to occur in the second trimester. The placenta then fails to provide the baby with sufficient nourishment, slowing the baby's growth.

The specialist immediately prescribed Fragmin, a blood thinner, which I had to inject into my thigh throughout the pregnancy. This was to prevent further clotting, which could have been fatal for both me and my baby.

Throughout the pregnancy, my baby was measuring small for dates, so I had to undergo regular Doppler scans. During the pregnancy, I discovered I was having a girl. I loved her from the moment I saw her on the scan.

Around that time, I was having prayer with a well-respected elderly pastor. He had extensive experience in the area of spiritual warfare and witchcraft. One day, he contacted me, saying that God had urgently placed it on his heart to pray with me. In his words, *"The coven wants your baby!"* His revelation shook me to my core. The constant spiritual battles I was experiencing drove me to prayer, pleading for God's protection over her. I shared this disclosure with my husband and my close friends.

A coven is an assembly or group of usually thirteen witches - a gathering of individuals with similar interests or activities.

FRUIT CAKE OR BEARING FRUIT

Because the baby was breech, a caesarean section was planned. The night before the operation, my husband helped me settle into a side room at the hospital and left around 9:30pm, planning to return the next morning at 9am. The Fragmin injections had to be stopped 24 hours before the procedure to prevent excessive bleeding during surgery.

However, at 11pm, I started having contractions. At first, I was confused - it had been eight years since my last pregnancy, and I didn't *want* to remember the pain. I prayed, *"Am I having contractions?"* In that moment, I noticed a sign on the wall that seemed to glow. It was a picture of a car seat with the inscription:

"A child is a precious gift - don't take any chances!"

I immediately pressed the panic button.

The midwife on duty rushed in, examined me, and announced that I was already 7cm dilated and that the baby was on the way. Suddenly, it was all systems go. The staff were in a frenzy, running everywhere.

Yet, in the midst of the chaos, I felt completely enveloped by an incredible peace, as if I were hovering above the bed with hands underneath me, watching everything unfold. I knew without a doubt that God was in control.

As I wouldn't be awake during the operation, I made a special request to the midwife: "Please put my baby straight to my breast. I want to feed her. And make sure you confirm that she's a girl - I don't want there to be any mix-ups."

Christine was born on 17th August, with a beautiful mop of jet-black hair. We chose her name from the word *to christen* - a baptism into the Christian faith.

When I came round from the anaesthetic, oddly, it wasn't my husband who was present but my mother. She told me she had tried to wake him by throwing stones at our house window. Strangely, our two dogs hadn't barked, and he hadn't heard the phone or the commotion - nothing at all.

I chose to breastfeed Christine for ten months. Looking back, I realise that decision was part of God's protection. My mother constantly pressured me to stop breastfeeding and switch to formula so that she could have Christine overnight. But something inside me resisted, and I kept breastfeeding. Now, I see that as an answered prayer, keeping Christine safe during that vulnerable time, as my relationship with my mother ended just before I stopped breastfeeding.

When Christine turned two, she wasn't weaning properly. Her development in walking and talking was delayed. Despite so many people around me reassuring me that everything was fine, God showed me otherwise.

FRUIT CAKE OR BEARING FRUIT

I sought further advice and, shortly after a referral to a specialist, Christine was diagnosed with autism and a learning difficulty.

Our journey with Christine is a story in itself, one that deserves its own book. I've decided to call it *Unique* because every stage of her development has revealed God's divine intervention.

Since then, many people have corroborated my disclosures. Some shared that there were individuals - now deceased - who had wanted to come forward and see me but were too afraid.

My grandfather was an MP and a *Worshipful Master* in the Masons. He passed his uniform down to another family member who was a policeman. What a tangled web.

There is only one Master we are to worship - Jesus, who said, "It is written:

Worship the Lord your God and serve him only.
(Luke 4:8)

Anything else is deception and the occult. The very word *occult* means *hidden*. The Masons are a *secret society*, but as Christians, we are called to walk in the light:

When Jesus spoke again to the people, he said, 'I am the light of the world. Whoever follows me will never walk in darkness but will have the light of life. (John 8:12).

Nothing is truly hidden, as Scripture tells us:

Nothing in all creation is hidden from God's sight. Everything is uncovered and laid bare before the eyes of Him to whom we must give account. (Hebrews 4:13).

My mother frequently contacted my friends and my husband's family, insisting I had *False Memory Syndrome* and that therapists had planted my memories there. I had so many flashbacks before I went for any therapy. She took videos around for them to watch, harping on about hypnosis being terrible - yet she had taken me for hypnosis herself! She was relentless in her efforts to undermine me. The family refused to watch the videos, as they believed me and found her behaviour deeply concerning.

One day, she called my close friend, who later told me about their conversation.

I had told my friend about my *many memories* of my grandmother dressing in a black cloak at Halloween and taking out her teeth. I also recalled a gathering of people in black cloaks at the local golf club and that my great-grandfather had been a magician and I had been told was in *The Black Magic Circle*.

FRUIT CAKE OR BEARING FRUIT

She mentioned these memories I was having to my mother.

My mother's response? She threatened to report me to social services as an unfit mother.

When my friend reported it back to me, that was the final straw.

That same evening, my mother called me again. This time, she asked if Jamie could come to her house to use her computer for his homework. I refused and said bluntly, *"No, because you told my friend that you're reporting me to social services as an unfit mother!"*

She fervently denied saying it and declared she was coming round immediately. Then she had the audacity to suggest that I should choose my friends more carefully. She arrived so quickly that I was sure she must have flown on a broomstick!

As soon as she entered, she went straight into the lounge to 'groom' my husband, as she had always done. I retreated to the kitchen, feeling the need to pray. Desperately, I cried out to God: *"If You're there, You're going to have to help me now!"*

In that moment, it felt as if a bolt of lightning struck me. Empowered, I walked straight into the lounge, pointed my finger firmly at my mother, and exclaimed, *"Enough!"*

At that command, she was propelled backwards onto the settee. The sight was gruesome - her lips stuck to her chattering teeth due to lack of saliva, her whole body shaking uncontrollably. Words of victory flowed from my mouth, as if from somewhere beyond me.

"Your control no longer works! Get back and tell them they're not big enough. Who are you going to run to now? The doctor? Oh, that didn't work. Your solicitor? The family? I am a Christian now, and I will tell the truth until I draw my last breath!"

She looked desperately at my husband and cried, "What are we going to do with her?"

I immediately drew my arm down between them, a symbolic act of breaking ungodly ties. "You can cut that out. He and I are united. You've always lied and tried to split us up."

She looked at me with the same manipulative expression she had used on me as a child. "Look at me when I'm speaking to you. You know your mum would never hurt you."

But it was over. Game over. The hypnotic trance, the mind control - it was all broken.

My husband went straight upstairs to be with the children who were ready for bed.

FRUIT CAKE OR BEARING FRUIT

In the heat of the moment, she suggested I go for prayer. I responded with disdain, "Who to? I wish you could just cross over, Mum. We are in different camps."

She left that night, and that was the end of our relationship. I had to shatter my "happy" picture of my mother in order to protect them - not just from her but from any others they might encounter in life who might do similarly. Knowledge is often power.

Afterwards, I ran to my husband and the boys, still reeling from what had just happened. "Was I weak?" I asked him, still dazed.

"Good grief, no. I've never seen anything like it!" he replied, astonished.

Things would never be the same after that night.

Years later, I read a chapter in Nicky Cruz's book, *One Holy Fire*. In it, he described how witches came to heckle at one of his meetings, and his windpipe became restricted.

The Holy Spirit instructed him to step off the stage and pray again. He felt Gods Anointing fall upon him and when he returned, he declared, "You've had your fun, Devil; now it's God's turn!" Stretching out his arm, he pointed his finger across the audience.

Witches immediately started screaming, some ran away, others fell to the floor and many came to the Altar in repentance to be saved.

As I read his account, God showed me that what happened to Nicky Cruz that day was exactly what had happened to me in the kitchen all those years ago. When I prayed for help against my mother's witchcraft, the same anointing of the Holy Spirit fell on me. It was the Spirit who led me to point the Finger of God at her, breaking the power of darkness and causing her to manifest demonic activity.

There is power in the name of Jesus. Amen.

Later I remembered when Mr and Mrs White and I prayed together for Christine whilst she was sleeping. I instantly felt an eerie, dark presence behind me and the hairs on the back of my neck stood up. As I pulled back the curtain there was a gift my mother had given her at her Christening, of a child kneeling and praying. I instantly destroyed it and threw it in the bin.

Chapter 10
God Promises, God Saves

Guilt is a burden I have often carried when it comes to my children. Sometimes we think we're protecting others by our silence when in actuality we may be causing more harm. However, God has assured me that they have the same pathway to freedom that I do - by seeking Him for their healing too.

I can happily say that laughter truly is like medicine. I've learned to laugh in the face of adversity. If you don't laugh, you cry, and I've cried enough to last a lifetime. God's Word is true, as it says in Nehemiah 8:10: *"The joy of the Lord is your strength."* Love's abiding joy has kept us strong on this journey to freedom.

The world says that beauty is only skin-deep, and I had so many wrinkles from stress and tears that I decided to see them as laughter lines instead. Today, I wholeheartedly agree with the Psalmist, who declared:

"You have turned for me my mourning into dancing" (Psalm 30:11).

I love to express my worship through dance. The more I focus on God, the more I find myself completely abandoned in praise, overflowing with gratitude for all He has done for me. "God's great dance floor," has become a wonderful place of freedom for me, where my heart pours out its adoration to Him. I've also come to understand that praise and worship are powerful weapons against the enemy. Oh, how I love to dance for the Lord, bringing down enemy strongholds as I do!

So many times, some Christians have tried to quench my dancing, but whenever that happens, God always sends someone to encourage me. They'll tell me they've encountered His anointing in a special way or even heard angels singing. That affirmation strengthens my resolve to keep being obedient to Him and dance on injustice.

As a Christian beauty therapist, I've come to appreciate the real beauty revealed in the heart through the connections and relational aspects of the body of Christ - the Church. This loving kindness has been shown to me so clearly through another steadfast friend who I met her at our local church. She had a young family too, so we had much in common.

FRUIT CAKE OR BEARING FRUIT

Whenever I was having a particularly bad day, she would show up unexpectedly. My first thought would often be, "Oh no, the God squad is here!" In those moments, I didn't always want to hear the truth because I was in such a difficult place. This friend and I would often walk the dog, and along the way, we'd see signs like "vertical access," "salt and grit," and "dark lane leading to the heights." These signs would symbolically lift our thoughts heavenward. As we talked about the Lord, my depression would lift, and hope would stir in my heart again.

Bless her, she was so faithful to me during those dark years when I was at my worst. She never doubted God's call on my life, even when others were sceptical.

From those walks of hope, *Fit for Life,* helping people become spiritually fit for life, was birthed at our Christian ministry beauty clinic. God spoke to us, saying He wanted us to share our experience of Him with others. We began by opening my home for a free lunch every week.

"Man looks at the outward appearance, but God sees the heart" (1 Samuel 16:7)

As a beauty therapist, I found myself increasingly drawn to promoting salvation over make-up foundation. Not that there's anything wrong with looking after ourselves, but when vanity becomes an obsession, it is counterproductive. I have realised that we have an identity crisis if it isn't found in Christ and His unconditional love for us. I began seeking God's guidance during my work, and He made it clear that I needed to change the way I was working.

One day, I was pondering what that change might look like when I came across a learner driver on the road. Their car had a sign on the back that read, "Please be patient." In that moment, I knew God was speaking to me.

That was my answer.

Gradually, I began introducing Christian music into the clinic. The atmosphere changed dramatically, and before long, I found myself praying with clients. Some of them gave their lives to the Lord right in the middle of facial massages or during manicures. Others opened up about deep issues that were troubling them.

I remember thinking, "I'm not a vicar - I can't even name the twelve disciples!" But God assured me that as long as I acknowledged Him, He would do the work of salvation.

During my journey with the local church, while still struggling with alcohol, I attended their house group Christmas party. They knew I was going to Alcoholics Anonymous meetings, yet they had alcohol at the party. I felt so hurt to be put in temptation's way. When I returned home, God led me to this scripture:

FRUIT CAKE OR BEARING FRUIT

Therefore let us stop passing judgment on one another. Instead, make up your mind not to put any stumbling block or obstacle in the way of a brother or sister. (Romans 14:13).

It was a pivotal moment for me. I realised that spiritual maturity is about putting others before ourselves and helping them not to stumble.

On Sunday evening, I went to visit a Baptist church to hear inspiring testimonies of people who had found freedom in Christ. I felt a deep calling to be baptised. Before approaching my local vicar to ask his permission, God gave me this scripture:

All this I have told you so that you will not fall away. They will put you out of the synagogue; in fact, the time is coming when anyone who kills you will think they are offering a service to God. They will do such things because they have not known the Father or me. I have told you this so that when their time comes you will remember that I warned you about them. (John 16:1-4).

When I asked the vicar to come to my full-immersion baptism, he sadly refused. He said that if I went through with it, I would need to leave the church, as they did not believe it was necessary. Thank goodness God had prepared me with that word. The rejection didn't cause me to lose faith.

I held onto the truth of Luke 3:16:

John answered them all, 'I baptise you with water. But one who is more powerful than I will come, the straps of whose sandals I am not worthy to untie. He will baptise you with the Holy Spirit and fire.

That evening, as I lay in my bath, I prayed, "Lord, what do You want me to do?" At that moment, the words on my shampoo bottle at the end of the bath seemed to light up: *"WASH AND GO."*

I chose to obey God, get baptised and left my local church.

Chapter 11
Ministry Flourishes

As my business blossomed, I felt the Holy Spirit enlightening me about people and church attendance. I realised that many people believe in God but don't go to church. They might watch religious programmes like *Songs of Praise* at home because they've been hurt in church or they're not feeling good enough to attend.

God led me to a verse in Luke 14 that paints a beautiful picture of a generous invitation to a dinner party:

> *"When you give a dinner or a supper, do not ask your friends, your brothers, your relatives, nor rich neighbours, lest they also invite you back, and you be repaid. But when you give a feast, invite the poor, the maimed, the lame, the blind. And you will be blessed, because they cannot repay you; for*

*you shall be repaid at the resurrection of the just."
(Luke 14:12–14).*

I believed this scripture confirmed the vision to open the doors of hospitality at our ministry. Even though I hadn't been to Bible College, I discerned that God was saying He wasn't looking for "religionists" but for "redeemers". I trusted that if we invited our "Unseen Guest" to be with us, He would guide us.

We would have a weekly 'Fit For Life' prayer meeting in the morning with the opportunity of sharing and caring. This was followed by an open house lunch.

This step of faith brought challenges I wasn't prepared for. I found myself watching people walk through my pristine, clean house with muddy shoes, dropping food on the floor. Often, guests would catch me on my knees under the kitchen table - not praying, but cleaning!

People would say, "Isn't she kind and generous," but they had no idea that all of this came about through obedience. God was teaching me the difference between being a steward and an owner of what He had given me.

Unsurprisingly, my husband and the boys didn't understand this truth at the time. They often made references to me giving away all the food while they were out "grafting." I had to endure their mocking and jokes about how I wasn't "working" in the way I used to. It wasn't easy. In my heart, I knew I was serving the Most High God, and while I longed for their approval, I didn't depend on it.

Each week, people would turn up. Some came through word of mouth, while others said they had walked past the shop, seen it "light up," and felt drawn to come in. Those moments were precious. I watched as people connected in amazing ways.

Those years were pivotal for me, "hedging me in" when circumstances were difficult. I couldn't escape - it was my home, but through it all, I saw the ministry grow. The Word prophesied many times over the ministry was that it was an 'Oasis in the desert' and a 'Watering hole'. How incredible to see that a place that once had been used to wash clothes physically was now being used to wash them spiritually. Twenty years on, it still thrives. After the first seven years, it even won a Pride Award fulfilling the prophecy that our Christian ministry would be a beacon for the Lord!

I gave all the glory to Him. I couldn't deny the signs and miracles that took place there.

Jesus says in John's Gospel:

And I, when I am lifted up from the earth, will draw all people to myself. (John 12:32).

God has been so true to His Word, assuring me that He has plans for my future - not to harm me, but to prosper me and give me hope and a future. Secure in Christ, it is a privilege to now see others encountering His love for them, witnessing answers to their prayers too, and praising the One who rescued me for His purposes and glory alone.

At one point, my late local MP asked me to appear on a well-known television programme with him to speak out on Satanic Ritual Abuse (SRA). The journalist leading the programme claimed it was intended to help social workers, who were under fire in the wake of several quashed cases. Wanting to help other children, I agreed to take part and went to the MP's house for filming.

My mother had been horrified and said, "You can't go on TV they might murder you and the children!"

I immediately responded with, "Who?"

To which she replied, "I know that it goes on but it hasn't happened to you."

How did she know that it goes on?

The Founder of Childwatch rang me shortly afterwards. She warned me that the programme was deceptive and not intended to help social workers at all but rather to deny the existence of SRA entirely. Alarmed, I immediately called them and asked to be removed from the programme. They ignored my request. When the programme aired, it showed other survivors whose faces were blacked out, keeping them anonymous. But they broadcast my full identity, with no care whatsoever for my safety.

I learned that the journalist responsible has been called out since for similar deceptive practices in a programme involving a very prominent person years later.

The late, great Dennis Wrigley was the founder of the Christian organisation *Maranatha*. He became a spiritual father to me. I had much encouragement and prayer support from the community, including other members. We held regular monthly meetings at the local nursery, which were such a blessing and well attended.

Dennis was speaking as a Christian voice in Parliament at the time. *Trumpet Call* was a regular letter sent out to members to pray and act on important issues affecting our nation. He wrote an article titled *What on Earth Are We Doing to Our Children?* I went to the House of Commons with him to speak out, and he invited me to appear on TV and the *Radio.*

After the *Radio* interview I was asked if I would leave my name for the viewers. I agreed, but on the drive home asked God if I had been wise in that decision. I immediately received confirmation when I drove past a building that had a sign on saying "YES". Shortly afterwards I received a call from someone who had listened to my interview and was a producer. He confided that he thought he was involved in something sinister. He described waking up with scratches and dirty feet, convinced he was being taken into the woods at night against his will. Was he, too, under mind control?

Dennis Wrigley was to later speak at my 50th birthday party - the year of Jubilee - and shared a word God had given him for me: "Dunamis", the power of God.

He proclaimed that the vision God had given me was like dynamite, capable of blowing up the enemy's camp!

Meanwhile, the police finally started to move forward with my case. They sent CID officers abroad to speak with my brother. During the interview, he admitted that our father had flown out to visit him beforehand and asked him to sign a form stating he hadn't abused me. My brother refused to sign it. The report from CID noted that my brother had "escaped the family" and chosen to live far away.

Later, senior officers requested a meeting with me. One night, the same female officer who had interviewed the two sisters picked me up in plain clothes for another interview. From the moment it began, I felt their hostility. Coldly, they asked, "How come it's taken you so long to come forward?"

Their lack of empathy made me feel like the perpetrator, not the victim. At the time I am sure the police may have been unaware of the fact that disclosure of CSA during childhood is often delayed. Indeed, current research from the National Institute for Health states : It is estimated that between 55% and 70% of those who experience sexual abuse as a child delay disclosure until adulthood ([London et al., 2008](#)). [Hébert et al. (2009)](#) found that as few as one in five disclosed CSA during childhood. Lengths of delay vary but have been reported as up to 60 years ([McElvaney, 2002](#)).

After several what felt like snide comments from these so-called officers, I felt an inner strength rise up within me.

"I've almost had a nervous breakdown once," I told them firmly. "I have told you the truth. If you choose to do nothing about this, then it is on your conscience, not mine. I have done my duty to safeguard children!"

From that moment, the police proceeded to plan a dawn raid on my father's 'house. Unfortunately, they were tipped off, and my father was conveniently away when they made their first attempt. The following week, they tried again and arrested him.

I had told the police about a cellar under the lounge carpet in my father's house, a detail my brother had disclosed to me. When the police investigated, the cellar was flooded with water. I later learned that Satanists often destroy evidence by fire or flood. That cellar was where much of the abuse had taken place.

The police told me they believed me but said they didn't have enough evidence to proceed further. They urged me to come forward again if anything else transpired.

Two years after my father's arrest, someone anonymously posted a newspaper article through my door that he was opening a 40-place children's day nursery next to his house.

They were clearly hoping I would do something about it. I was horrified. I wrote to social services, pointing out that there had been enough evidence to arrest him, so how on earth could he now have access to children? What qualifications did he have to open a Children's Nursery I wondered? They thanked me for bringing it to their attention and said that they hoped that I would be of service to them in the future. They sent the Head of Child Protection at the time, Drake Wheeler, to visit me at my home.

When he arrived, I could sense his cautious approach. We had a truthful conversation, and by the end, he said, "Before I came, I thought you were either barking mad or telling the truth. Now that I've met you, I believe the latter!"

I couldn't help but laugh and showed him a recent wedding anniversary card I had on the kitchen windowsill. It featured a picture of a dog and a duck and read,

"I think you're barking mad, and you think I'm quackers!" God really does have a sense of humour!

Drake went back to one of his officers, DC Kate McIntyre, who he said was so excited to take on my case. They sent a psychologist to assess whether I was strong enough to attend court, who reported back that I was, and estimated that the trial would be approximately 12–18 months away.

All they needed was my brother to confirm that our father had flown out after I had disclosed to visit him and asked him to sign a form denying the abuse. My brother had already refused to sign it, and his admission was on record.

But then, out of nowhere, DC Kate McIntyre went off sick, and Drake Wheeler announced his retirement. The case was closed again.

The police finally called me in again for another interview with senior officers to have an assessment with one of their forensic psychiatrists even though they had previously sent one to my home. Thankfully,

God had forewarned me. I brought a solicitor to the meeting, and because of that preparation, they were unable to try and section me – which is what I felt they were trying to do. In the psychiatrists report however he says that I have been abused.

Years later, I crossed paths again with DC Kate McIntyre at the health club we both attended. She apologised to me, explaining that she had been seriously unwell during my case and had taken early retirement due to the politics within the force.

Chapter 12
Eagles Nest

After many disappointing package holidays and more than a few allergic reactions to the sun, we decided to get a touring caravan. We had some lovely holidays in Devon, but eventually, we parked it up permanently in Wales for a season. However, the caravan site had no amenities in bad weather, and the journey there - especially during peak times - was exhausting, with endless traffic jams.

Determined to find a holiday park closer to home, I wanted a place that felt familiar, somewhere we could return to regularly. We had been members of a health club since Christine was five, so I hoped to find a caravan site with similar activities. This was essential, as autism thrives on routine, and it would also be easier for me to manage when my husband was away.

I prayed and, when Christine was 13, found a wonderful place not too far away, with plenty to do.

We traded in our tourer for a reasonably priced static at Eagle's Nest.

When we moved in, I hadn't been able to get my favourite coffee and had to settle for another brand. Upon arrival, as I opened the empty cupboards, I found one that wasn't empty at all. Inside was a jar of the very same favourite brand! I burst into tears, knowing this was yet another sign of God's favour on my life. It was the start of a new chapter, full of treasured memories in our holiday home.

Not long after, I felt the Lord ask me, "Are you prepared for me to blow you to The Nest, out of the serpent's way?" He led me to this scripture:

The wind blows wherever it pleases. You hear its sound, but you cannot tell where it comes from or where it is going. So, it is with everyone born of the Spirit. (John 3:8-9)

Around the same time, I came across a school for autism in the area and felt it would be a wonderful place for Christine to experience childhood. As I surrendered to God's voice, everything started to fall into place. I was in desperate need of respite, and looking back, I now see the deeper meaning of the words *"out of the serpent's way."* Once again, God led me to scripture:

FRUIT CAKE OR BEARING FRUIT

The woman was given the two wings of a great eagle, so that she might fly to the place prepared for her in the wilderness, where she would be taken care of for a time, times and half a time, out of the serpent's reach. (Revelation 12:14-15)

It was another *Godincidence* - not only had He brought us to a caravan at Eagle's Nest, but our address was No 21. The number 21 also signifies *"key to the door"* and connected to another scripture He gave me:

These are the words of him who is holy and true, who holds the key of David. What he opens no one can shut, and what he shuts no one can open. (Revelation 3:7-10)

This was truly a place of spiritual safety. By then, the boys were grown up and stayed at home with Chris during the week, visiting at weekends.

God told me I would live there for three winters, and sure enough, we returned home when Christine was 16. During that time, He did a deep work in my life - teaching me how to be comfortable in my own skin, even in solitude. I found a wonderful local church and made many dear friends.

The Lord also told me to start *Fit For Life* at the caravan and revealed that a close friend, at our church, would run it with me. Before I even asked her, a gentleman at church confirmed it, saying that she had always been his *"Oasis in the desert"* - the exact phrase spoken over the ministry of *Fit For Life* previously. She agreed, and we had many blessed meetings, creating memories to cherish.

Another friend, a true prayer warrior, was also instrumental in encouraging me to keep walking in faith. Once, when I had a police interview - yes, those were still happening even while I lived away - she had a dream. She saw me on a water ride at a fairground, getting on the boat to be carried across to the other side, drenched in water, with many people queuing behind me. This was symbolic of the people who would come to know Jesus and be baptised into the Christian faith as they heard my story. I must continue to trust and obey.

I also attended a church house group led by a woman really grounded in the word of God, where we studied *Heirs of the Prophets*. It revealed to me that *there is nothing new under the sun* - that the same evils that existed in Old Testament times are still present today. As God is the same yesterday and forever, so is the devil. It confirmed what I already knew about my childhood, despite so many still refusing to believe that witchcraft is real.

FRUIT CAKE OR BEARING FRUIT

Christine and I later became part of another fellowship and the leaders there have become lifelong friends who have pastored and supported us ever since.

God's plan was unfolding, and as always, His hand was over our lives.

Exactly 3 years later, as God had said, we returned home.

Chapter 13
Uncovered Memories

As my mind continued to thaw, more memories continued to surface. I recalled as a child being taken out at night and being told to stand next to a large tunnel on my left with people in black cloaks chanting on my right. My back was against a cold, hard wall with a reservoir in front of me with a black cloak floating on the water. I recall hearing screaming and the memory of that still affects me today.

When I was at primary school living at my grandmother's house, I woke up to seeing nothing but long legged spiders crawling all over my wallpaper with no space between them. It was a result of being given hallucinogenic drugs when they took me out at night to the rituals – I assume so that I wouldn't remember what happened there. They were all forms of demonic bondage using hypnosis as well.

VICKY ASH

We had collection boxes in our home for the children who were in care in our area. We referred to them as the orphanage children and my father often visited them with gifts.

I also remember seeing children, that we didn't know, coming up to my father's house when I was there with my brother. I was wearing my school summer uniform.

When I went away on summer holiday with my father he entered me into a fancy dress competition as Lady Godiva. I had to walk around at the approximate age of ten in just a pair of knickers and I remember winning a huge chocolate bar. I heard recently, with horror, that one of my relatives had a collection of pornography called 'Godiva Girls'.

On those holidays my father would always duck me under the water when swimming and hold me under. He would insist again and again that I had to dive off the top board which was very high. I absolutely hated diving as the water always went up my nose and I would do 'belly flops' and my tummy would be red raw. He got pleasure out of me being hurt and offered to give me money to do it.

Early teens at my father's house outside at night in front of the Infirmary the Satanists crowded round me in their cloaks with all their hands coming towards me chanting, "She's sinned … she's sinned …. Punish her … Punish her!"

This was a trigger when I first started going to Church hearing the word "sin".

God brought me to full healing by bringing revelation of His Word in my adult years ….

There is no fear in love. But perfect love drives out fear, because fear has to do with punishment. The one who fears is not made perfect in love. (1 John 4:18 | NIV)

We can see from this how Satan perverts scripture to keep victims in deception and bondage.

In my twenties I can remember my father taking a homeless man off the streets and giving him his clothes to wear that didn't fit him properly. His relative remarked how kind he was doing this but I just saw this man having to do lots of jobs for him almost like a servant.

Age 25, I drove up to my father's house and saw one of his sheep in the mortuary field with its stomach ripped open (it's lamb had been removed) …. my father told me that a dog had attacked it. This wasn't true as they sacrifice animals in their rituals (hence why he owned 'very good looking sheep' and always remarked that they had bottoms like a woman!) A relative commented to me that he thought my father had sex with them!

In the outhouse there would always be sheep's heads on the worktop that they said were from the butchers for their Alsatian dog.

In my early teens I recall being taken down into the cellar at my father's house and a man being between my legs performing an abortion ... I was pregnant. After this recollection I telephoned the gynaecologist who had surgically removed my cyst to ask if he could tell if I had previously had an abortion. He said that he wouldn't have known if I had. Breeders are part of Satanism they impregnate the women in the coven and abort the babies for sacrifice to the devil. Why are we now seeing laws to legalise abortion at any stage and also lowering the age of consent to sex which is, in my opinion, legalising paedophilia?

> *For you were once darkness, but now you are light in the Lord. Live as children of light (for the fruit of the light consists in all goodness, righteousness and truth) and find out what pleases the Lord. Have nothing to do with the fruitless deeds of darkness, but rather expose them. It is shameful even to mention what the disobedient do in secret. But everything exposed by the light becomes visible - and everything that is illuminated*

becomes a light. This is why it is said: "Wake up, sleeper, rise from the dead, and Christ will shine on you." Be very careful, then, how you live - not as unwise but as wise, making the most of every opportunity, because the days are evil. (Ephesians 5:8-17a | NIV)

These are my memories that I believe clearly now corroborate Satanism and their practices of Ritual Abuse in my life.

Family lies and treachery are revealed that almost destroyed me in my search for truth.

I did a lie detector test which of course I passed and showed to the police. I asked members of my family to take one also but they declined.

Another investigator who wanted to help with my case asked to have the lie detector test to copy and said that he would promptly return it to me. When it didn't arrive back, he said that he had sent it but it must have got lost in the post. Years later when he was being interviewed for the Independent Inquiry into Child Sexual Abuse (IICSA), I suddenly got an email that he had found it and returned it to me.

Chapter 14
Letting Go

My mother once said that my children would grow up with the shame of knowing that their mother had been Satanically Ritually Abused my response to her was that no, they would grow up respecting the fact that I had done something about it.

Many people at Church said that forgiveness meant that I should still be in a relationship with my family that fervently denied my abuse. On the contrary, God clearly showed me that reconciliation could only come with true repentance. That includes our personal reconciliation to God and in relationships particularly ones that involve abuse.

This scripture came to mind again ….

What harmony is there between Christ and Belial? Or what does a believer have in common with an unbeliever? What agreement is there between the temple of God and idols? For we are the temple of the living God. As God has said: "I will live with them and walk among them, and I will be their God, and they will be my people." Therefore, "Come out from them and be separate, says the Lord. Touch no unclean thing, and I will receive you." And, "I will be a Father to you, and you will be my sons and daughters," says the Lord Almighty. (2 Corinthians 6:15-18)

As part of my therapy and still in my 'childlike state' I returned to visit my father at his place of work to say, "I'm sorry for telling." His response was to quickly usher me away from anyone in ear shot.

He had a letter opener in his hand and turned it towards his chest saying, "You may as well have stabbed me here with what you have done to me, if you want to resume a relationship with me you need to go and tell everyone that I haven't done it." I responded by saying "I'm not here to resume a relationship, I've just come to apologise for telling the truth so that I can heal. I felt another chain break as I drove away free from his control.

This separation also became clear to me after the birth of my first grandson. His parents took a beautiful picture of all their hands inside each other showing the next generation.

FRUIT CAKE OR BEARING FRUIT

When leaving a Church service one Friday morning I was deliberating over my mother's requests by letter, yet again, to see him. Whilst driving home a song came on called 'We Cry Out' and the lyrics hit me:

"We are a chosen generation, oh yes, a generation that's free ..."

The picture of those hands came up on my phone. God was showing me clearly not to as he had set my family and the next generation FREE!

I know in my heart that I have truly forgiven those who hurt me but I will never jeopardise the safety of my immediate family.

My husband and I are now settled at a wonderful community church, and we can see that *The Kingdom* jigsaw is finally coming together in these days. Our whole family attend their monthly Messy Church which is described as a way of being church for families and others. It is Christ-centred, for all ages, based on creativity, hospitality and celebration.

I didn't realise, before I was led to go, that some of the leaders there had prayed with me many, many years ago at the beginning of my Christian journey and can now witness the fruit of their prayers in my life.

Some of the ladies at our current church are also part of a group I am involved in called *Christian Women of Influence (CWOI)*, led by Pastor Innocentia

Ezeh. She is very experienced in the area of teaching deliverance ministry within the body of Christ and carries God's anointing to set captives free. We are truly blessed to be part of her ministry.

Whilst attending Healing Stream I had a vision of a well opening up in the floor of our meeting room at our ministry gushing out into the world beyond. The water continued to pour out because its source is God Himself. He spoke clearly to me saying that this water constituted the tears of the children and also the tears of the saints who have earnestly prayed. God is now opening up ancient wells all across our nation in these end times.

The world is now *waking up* to the reality of Satanic Ritual Abuse as thousands of survivors are speaking out across the nations. God's Church is the answer to rescue those victims and survivors.

There are many witnesses to the events that have happened that have spoken out on my behalf and given statements to the police. Witnesses continue to contact me to validate my case.

The purpose of writing this book is certainly not for revenge. Those who abused me know who they are. I pray that they come to the place of true repentance and salvation as I have.

The Bible clearly says ….

Do not take revenge, my dear friends, but leave room for God's wrath, for it is written: "It is mine to avenge; I will repay," says the Lord. On the contrary: "If your enemy is hungry, feed him; if he is thirsty, give him something to drink. In doing this, you will heap burning coals on his head." Do not be overcome by evil, but overcome evil with good." (Romans 12 v 19-21)

On the contrary I have written it to educate those who deny the existence of SRA in order to protect and save children.

Chapter 15
Hope and Glory

Anyone who has ever been sexually abused should never feel ashamed. In the book of Romans, chapter 8, it says:

Therefore, there is now no condemnation for those who are in Christ Jesus. (Romans 8:1).

There is no guilt, no condemnation - it was not our fault. That's why I can share my story so openly, to help others find freedom without fear of man or seeking man's approval.

A question I'm often asked is: "Why does a loving God let bad things happen to good people?"

What helped me was understanding the truth, in Romans, chapter 3:

For all have sinned and fall short of the glory of God. (Romans 3:23)

The truth is, none of us are good enough, because God is holy. It took the sacrifice of His Son, Jesus, on the cross to atone for all sin and bring us back into a relationship with the Living God.

Throughout my journey of faith, God has proven Himself faithful in every promise He has ever made in His Word. He redeemed my life from the pit, and I can now declare, just as it says in Psalm 40:

He put a new song in my mouth, a hymn of praise to our God. Many will see and fear the Lord and put their trust in him. (Psalm 40:3)

From the day I made Jesus my Lord and Saviour, He has been prophetically restoring the years that the locusts have eaten - the years I lost to deception and abuse - as described in Joel 2:25. I am now walking in hope and prospering in the future He promised in Jeremiah 29:11. I've learned that His grace has always been sufficient in my weakness, and I owe Him my life.

God did not abuse me. It was our adversary, the Devil, who orchestrated that pain. The Devil goes on killing, stealing, and destroying lives, being the liar that he is, hoping that God, who truly loves us, gets the blame and that our faith is destroyed.

When we are in trouble, we must run to God, like the prodigal son did, to be saved and reconciled with the Father. God never wants anyone to go to Hell -

that's why He sent Jesus to save us. He gives us free will to choose Him or not.

My earthly father betrayed me, but my Heavenly Father fought for me and won the battle at Calvary. My name itself reflects the outcome of this battle, showing me that I am greatly loved by Him.

In that victorious overcoming, I now stand firm, believing what Jesus said:

With man this is impossible, but with God all things are possible. (Matthew 19:26)

Today, I believe Jesus could be looking at you as you face your own impossibility. Today, you could walk into His victory.

I pray that after reading my story, you will be inspired to seek God with all your heart and find Him. In doing so, you will discover the only life worth living - His life in you, the Hope of Glory.

God bless you.

Last Word

Our problems in Britain began with the abolishing of the Witchcraft Act in 1951 when the occult (which means hidden) was then legalised. This is why we see our laws rapidly changing.

Woe to those who call evil good and good evil, who put darkness for light and light for darkness, who put bitter for sweet and sweet for bitter. (Isaiah 5:20-21)

Satanic Ritual Abuse (SRA) is the practising of the rituals involved in the ideology of Satanism. The Bible clearly tells us that ultimately it will be the religion of The One World Order and the coming of the Antichrist who substitutes himself in Christ's place before the Second Coming of Jesus Christ.

It was given power to wage war against God's holy people and to conquer them. And it was given authority over every tribe, people, language and nation. All inhabitants of the earth will worship the

beast - all whose names have not been written in the Lamb's book of life, the Lamb who was slain from the creation of the world.
Whoever has ears, let them hear.
(Revelation 13:7-9)

Hope, however, has a name and His name is Jesus.

Acknowledgements

I would not be here without Jesus Christ but I also wouldn't be here without the numerous people He has divinely placed in my life.

I am grateful to all who have supported me throughout, in many different ways. Here I would like to give special thanks to those whose help and friendship have been significant in enabling me to produce this account, which I pray will help others on their restorative journey in Christ so that they too may "bear much fruit".

With great appreciation, I would like to honour:

My immediate family - my husband and three awesome children - who, despite much adversity, are witnessing the faithfulness of God and experiencing the restoration of the years the locusts have eaten, as promised in the book of Joel.

My sisters-in-law and their families for standing by me and being a constant source of comfort.

Janet and Tony for their faithful ministry and my wider Church family - the pastors and leaders.

My campaigning brothers and sisters in CASRA.

Jon Wedger, ex Scotland Yard detective campaigning for justice for victims, exposing an establishment cover up of child abuse who I have had the privilege of doing numerous interviews and podcasts with over the years.

My awesome friends - Pascale, Sarah, Gail, Margaret, Doreen, Michelle, Mark, Louise, Rachael, Sandrine, Sam, Charissa, Val and all who have not been mentioned who have been instrumental on my journey with Christ and encouraged me to keep on walking into my destiny.

All the intercessors, you know who you are, who have faithfully prayed for me throughout all these years. I love you all and am eternally grateful.

God Bless

Vicky

Printed in Great Britain
by Amazon